MW01119902

How to Paint Landscapes

OLIVIA KOSMO

Tellwell Talent
www.tellwell.ca

ISBN
978-0-2288-9343-1 (Hardcover)
978-0-2288-9342-4 (Paperback)
978-0-2288-9344-8 (eBook)

Table of Contents

*To my mom, for teaching me that I already
am who I've always wanted to be,
To my high school English teacher Amy Helsby,
for cultivating my passion for writing, and for
teaching me that feminism is not a dirty word,
And to every girl like me who believes she will never
be free: be your own saviour and just keep writing.*

The Easel

Art comes in so many forms
Only when it speaks to you
Does it reveal its true beauty

~ Masterpieces live in your mind

The marble steps I sat on during
the ceremony were ice cold
Just like your decision to marry her
six months after your divorce
If you could abandon the woman who
loved you for a decade of your life
For immediate submission and mindless obedience
What chance did I have of getting you to love me?

The first question I ever asked was,
"What's my name and how do you spell it?"
Because even then
I knew how to hang onto a constant
In an environment swirling with chaos

~ Grounded

When you grow up
Listening to the same insults
To the same argument put on a loop
All you are ever going to know
Are the words you have been told
And after a while
You start to believe them

~ When you wonder why I get so defensive

When I was five years old
A singer was my aspiration
I loved the sound of my voice
Certain and powerful
I used to belt out lyrics
As if I were the one who wrote them
Until you told me to be quiet
Silence is the only sound a girl should make
Compliance is the only passion a girl should have
Obedience is the only skill a girl should practice
I stopped singing
Thirteen years later
I have rediscovered this powerful voice of mine
But instead of using my vocals
to express my emotions
I use my pen

When you picked me up
And threw me in the air when I was five
The thrill excited me
It gave me goosebumps
I flew without wings and soared without gravity
What I didn't notice
Was the look in your eyes as you
gave me your warning
To never make you angry
While I was suspended between fun and fatality
I knew if I did you would have let me down hard
The same way you have for years now
After my head hit the ceiling
It became clear you wanted me to stop talking
Now as I rub the indent in the back of my skull
I understand what you taught me
I know that my silence started at a very young age
And that my fear was instilled from infancy

Lucky
I'm so lucky to have you
So lucky that you take every opportunity
to show me I'm worthless
To show me I'm unworthy
Of your respect or anyone else's
To show me how to take your
constant emotional blows
Or how to disintegrate my boundaries
Or rehearse my answer when someone asks how I am
Well if I'm so lucky to have you
Why do I shudder at the thought of your voice?
Why do I cry on the train ride to visit?
Why do I panic when the phone starts to ring?
If I am so lucky
Why do I feel so much pain?

What happens when the arms that
you were supposed to run into
When the wind picked up and the rain got heavy
Bare hurricanes and tidal waves worse than
any storm you could ever imagine?

I wore your shoes when I was a little girl
To be more like you
You scowled at me
And told me to put them back
That says it all right there
You don't even like yourself
So how could you ever love me?

I go to bed starving every night
When I know you have a twelve course
dinner locked up in the fridge
If only I could find the key

~ Hungry for affection

My head aches like a spine after 24
hours of manual labour
Incessant and relentless pounding ensue
As if someone in chains desires to break free
Your words echo through my mind
Deafening and excruciatingly painful
Please
I beg you
For even one second of silence

I yell and scream
To make you hear
How much you hurt me
How deep the pain runs through my veins
I shout until my throat aches and my lungs burn
Until my voice no longer carries
and my larynx goes numb
My raw emotion lacerates my innocence
and strips me of my immaturity
But still you look at me with a blank stare
And ask me why I am in such distress
After I lose my voice
I realize too late
That the walls blocking your capacity for empathy
Were soundproof all along

Kisses and hugs mean nothing
When you batter and bruise me with your tongue

Sometimes I wish I could scratch out the words I've spoken with a fountain pen

I felt your frigid fingers
Wrap themselves around my heart
As you presented me with a pencil and some foolscap
You told me to choose
There was always a right answer
But it was never an option

~ Multiple choice

My stomach aches so strongly to be rid of my anxiety
Just as the ocean floor begs to be warmed
by the rays of the midday sun
Tell me
Will the sand ever escape the darkness?

Not only do butterflies flutter when
my palms start to sweat
But bees swarm the hives they've built in my stomach
Wasps raid the picnic that was
supposed to calm me down
And moths fold themselves into tiny little triangles
Slipping themselves discreetly into my ears
They drink the rays of my inner light
Leaving me alone in the darkness
Anxiety is made of mosquitoes and moose flies
And I've left my swatter at home

~ Pests

No girl should have to live with her
elbows glued to her sides
So tightly it leaves bruises on her hips
And an ache so deep she winces when she moves
Just because her father will not stop touching her
She should not have to pray
For personal space

A knock requires an answer before an action
Because when I was nine and I said *don't come in*
I'm naked
But the door flew open anyway
I realized then that you never come to a full stop
Every time that little red sign appears
at the end of our intersection

~ Failed driving lessons

How fucked up do you have to be to question
if your whole existence is even worth it?

Every time I hear the word *father*
My tectonic plates start to shift
Slowly pushing against each other
Tension builds
Dirt cracks
Buildings crumble
I can already feel the Richter scale malfunctioning

~ He was an earthquake

Don't be the reason
Your daughter can't sleep at night
Don't be the reason
That your daughter shudders
At the thought of men
Or the reason
She weeps
When she hears the word *daddy*
Don't be the reason
Your daughter doesn't smile in pictures
Or that she feels empty
Deprived of joy
Roaming through the valleys of her mind
Searching for an escape
From the endless despair you have caused her
I beg you
Please
Don't do it
Just love her
It's all she wants
It's all she wants

You can't overturn my life sentence of incarceration
And then get angry
When I embrace recidivism like an old friend

~ My prison cell is my home

The Paintbrushes

My craving for freedom runs so deep
That the ocean gets down on its knees to worship me
Every night before it goes to bed

You don't tell me I'm nothing
You show me
And your actions say more
Than your speech ever could

~ Those three words are always empty

If only we could see
The condition of the spirit
Instead of the body
Because even though
My face is unmarked
My soul is black and blue

~ The battles fought silently are the most impactful

To constantly feel so deeply is a curse and a blessing
Which form it takes depends on the actions of others

She squeezes the half lemon until the
juice runs down her fingers
Like rain on a wheelbarrow
The acid from the liquid burns her cuticle
Seeping into a cut she didn't know she had
She keeps squeezing it anyway
After all
Who else is going to make the lemonade?

~ How to stay miserable

Those cherries you shoved down my throat
Choked me until I gagged
But poison often looks delicious
Especially when you're starving
You nourished me with a death sentence
Disguised as a snack
But I gobbled it up just the same
Hungry for more as tears ran down my cheeks
Stuffed with false promises and believable lies
Big scary smiles always taste like cherries
And my lips pucker at the familiar flavour
I am careful of the fruit I pick now
And I refuse to digest more than I can swallow

~ Cyanide poisoning

You say I look so much like your sister
I look in the mirror
I can't see it
Then I realize
You are telling me to be more like her
Because who I am
Is not good enough
It's too vivacious
It makes you angry
To see that I am my own person
To see that I look nothing like you or her
Strikes a chord with your hubris
Because I am happy
And she is miserable
You try to make me miserable too
But when I combat your efforts
It drives you crazy
Look at me
I will never be her
I will never be reduced to her
I will never be miserable

When you're in that apartment building
Trapped under that roof
Looking frantically to every closed door
What he tells you seems to be true
You can't see the hope of leaving
In a room locked from the outside

~ Keep searching for the key

Incessant terrorism reigns superior
I don't feel anything anymore
When you show me all the ways I don't matter
It's getting harder to combat your criticisms
When they have slowly become my own thoughts

~ Desensitization

I scrub my head absentmindedly
In circles I run my fingers through my hair
Hoping to wash away what has hurt me
I crave the boundaries
Of the locked door and running
water throughout the day
The paradoxical complex
Of being the most vulnerable
And the most secure
In the company of the soap and shampoo
Gives me uninterrupted peace
I can bathe in the poison of society all day long
But I wash it all away the second I turn on the faucet
I know I can always go back to
my glass box of serenity
And watch the weight I carry
disappear down the drain

~ In the shower

In my culture
To have a sense of individuality
Is the worst crime you could commit
You are part of a collective
Do not embarrass your family
By trying to be happy

~ Olives and oregano

I should not have to beg for life
Just let me live

Why have I always been afraid
when men are in the room
Intimidated and fearful is my initial reaction
Because since I got here
You taught me my place
In the corner is where you belong
But on stage is where I am
It is where I deserve to be
And I will never leave

~ Hand me the microphone

You were the cold to the lens in my glasses
Temporary
But ever so blinding

Oh to be blissfully naive while
you walk down the street
With your head held high and a smile upon your face
How I wish that could be me again

~ Lost innocence

My poor past self
She wasn't prepared
For the strike of a cast iron frying pan to the head
She couldn't see the light shining upon her
face when she neared the daylight hour
All she could do was simply stare at the
canvas painted completely black
As the intricate gold and paisley
picture frame became invisible
Only after she realized she had her
own acrylics and brushes
Could she see a different painting emerge
Now she finally realizes that her walls deserve art
And that she is more than worthy of landscapes

Five syllables
Four words
Three spaces
Two seconds
One person
"I don't believe you"
That's all it takes
To break my heart

~ Never say it

He tried to break you
Tear you to shreds
Strip you of yourself
Like a snake sheds its skin
But you left
For that alone
You deserve the world
So this is me
Giving you all of your flowers
You possess the strength of 10,000 female warriors
Carry your sword with pride

~ Battle armour

The world has been cruel to you
Robbed you of your essence
But every time I look at you
All I see is divinity
Don't ever let them take you
For you are a goddess
Masquerading as a woman

~ The brightest stars were once
told to dim their lights

Your words form a ladder
I use each sentence as a rung and climb
until my fantasies are tangible
Thank you for your words of encouragement
Without you there is no way I could
have gotten to the top

~ Mom

What is life
If you don't savour every breath you take
Regardless of whether it's shaky or smooth?

The Acrylics

How could you stare directly into my eyes
As wide as the horizon at the edge of an ocean
And still have the nerve to spill oil in my tide?

That look in your eye
Tells me
That you're the predator
And I'm the prey
But just because I look like a sheep
It doesn't mean
I can't bite like a wolf

~ Appearances can be deceiving

I have never cried in front of you
But just this one time
I thought if you could swim into the depths
Of my waters
You could see the damage you caused
To my coral reef

~ I don't know if your tears were genuine

They say the eyes are the windows to the soul
What does it mean
When I look into yours
And see nothing?

~ Apathy

You are an empty glass
That was never filled
With a single ounce of humanity

~ Thirsty for respect

They say to always write what you know
Never stray from familiarity
For it is always intertwined with
passion and eloquence
But when the back of your hand only looks like pain
And all you see is darkness when you close your eyes
It becomes inevitable
That the words beneath the pen
will always make tears fall

~ If you wonder why all my poems are so sad

He was the hammer
To my piece of glass
I may be shattered
But I will never be broken

What if we got paid to experience pain?
Each time measured
Weighed in emotional damage
A scale from a scrape to a stab
The amount in dollars would
equal how broken you feel
For if my pain was worth money
I would be as prosperous and wealthy
As a white man who goes through life
Without any consequences to his actions

He pulled every last string of breath from my lungs
Until they became threadbare
I thought he would stop sewing
When he used my heart as a pin cushion
But I guess his blanket needed more yarn

~ Quilt of despair

My teacher tells me
I could improve my writing
By being more succinct
But my trauma tells me
To keep talking until somebody listens

~ There should be no page limits to assignments

Even though I will always be proud of the heritage
I will forever be ashamed of the culture

~ It's not an excuse for your prejudice

What a terrible feeling it is
To know that your tongue will not dance
With the language it was assigned
She rejects the vernacular without question
When the foreign stranger so
eagerly offers her his hand

They will never tell you that there
are monsters among us
Walking freely down the street
Smiling at fellow pedestrians
And mingling with unsuspecting civilians
Luring them in with their false effervescence
Until what you once thought of as
perfect morphs into petrifying
Their mask has fooled you
You are caught between chaos and confusion
Convenience and coparenting
Cruelty and compassion
They have caught you in their trap
And now you'll always be their fly
Beware of the monsters
They silently walk among us

You never know when you've been gaslit
Until they've already lit the match and
the candle has started to burn
Dripping wax onto your favourite satin nightgown
Until every single thread that once brought you joy
Sizzles and turns to ash
Soon you begin to realize
You can never make the candle stop burning
Unless you choose to become the wind

When you are immersed in toxicity
You are bound to become poisoned
Leaving is the only remedy

~ Easier said than done

You are the darkness to my ray of sun
Never question why I chose the light

The Palette

Sometimes to lose someone
Is to release the shackles
Which bind you
To a life of misery
Only when the chain links break
Will you discover the person
Beneath the victim

Why is it
That whenever I am at my lightest
Darkness always comes stomping
through the back door?

~ Lock up when you leave

They say you can never make it
out of the fire unscathed
Only now do I realize how true this is
Just when I think I'm alright
Finally out of the blaze
That has scorched me for so long
I feel the ghost of your flames

What he left I took from myself
He threw out my lamp shades and
cut down my curtains
But I tore up the floorboards and
damaged the drywall
I changed the lock and let the food in the fridge spoil
I threw my bed out the window
And my couch off the roof
I thought I had gone crazy
But I was just tearing down so I could rebuild
After all
I am my own home
I might as well try to redecorate

You don't look broken to me
That's because you weren't there when I shattered
Super glue can only hold so much together
The only times when the pieces start to chip away
Are when I'm alone in my room
When the door is locked and my sobs are silent
So if you think you can determine the
state of my pottery at a single glance
I invite you to look closer
And see the cracks in my clay that were there
Long before you stepped into the museum

Validation is the reconstruction
of my dilapidated soul
Each person who expresses belief in my experiences
Is one brick put back into place
In the wall of sanity and rejuvenation

~ It takes a village to repair what was broken

Sometimes I fear the brightness in my eyes
will never return to its full wattage

Spider webs and dust cover the memories
Like an old book in a deserted library
Never to be visited again
But every once in a while
The door creaks open
The light shines in
And the library comes alive
The words between those pages are a tragedy
That should never be reread
It's only when I close the novel
That I know the feeling of regret
But will I do it again?
Of course

I look to the past so much I'm surprised
I haven't gotten whiplash

I deserve happiness
Happiness is attainable
I am deserving of peace
I am a good person
I am free to possess peace of mind

~ Affirmations

There is no greater form of psychological torture
than crying over a problem that doesn't exist
~ OCD

I didn't just break my own heart
I studied it
Made a blueprint
Stocked up weapons and took inventory
I ripped off tiny little pieces one
at a time with my fingers
Just so I could smash them with a sledgehammer
Slash them with a machete
Shatter them with a mallet
I took my time
Meticulous and ruthless and cruel
as I bashed and brutalized it
Until it looked nothing like my heart
Only an organ dismembered and
destroyed beyond repair
Scattered in pieces in an empty room
with a locked door and no windows
Begging for me to stop letting it beat
So the next time you think you can hurt me
Or get the urge to throw a stone at my glass exterior
Just to watch me break
Don't even waste your time
I've done enough smashing on my own

I'm sick of falling in love with being uncomfortable

When someone tells me I'm pretty
I just say thank you
And shake my head as they walk away
I look in the mirror when I get home to
see what they thought was so special
But I just don't see it
All I see is a body and a face
With a thousand mistakes that the
universe forgot to correct
Before it sent me down to Earth
If only it could finish what it started
Instead of just submitting a rough draft

I bid you 1000 apologies
For how much reassurance I will need
I must be the most aggravating person to tolerate
For to be my friend
Is to repeat yourself over and over
Until I realize your sincerity

~ He taught me to never believe your compliments

If only there was a way to burn sage inside of me
If only I could smoke my body up like a bonfire
Can I devour a sage stick?
Can I make a tea from it and gulp
it down like chocolate milk?
How can I get the smoke to
permeate my subconscious?
That's the place where it really needs to be
To breathe in that smoke is the best I can do
But I worry it won't ever be enough

I wish there were a physical remedy
for internal damage
A spiritual Gravol to pop when my energy is tainted
I squirm in my skin and my mind goes numb
I wish my stomach would not offend so easily
When poisonous words enter my subconscious
They also hit me in the abdomen
Uncomfortable and constant
They love to make themselves at home
In the pit of my stomach
Eating me from the inside
Devouring my contentment
I need some sort of soulful medication
I need to be surrounded by positivity
I just need peace

I've spilled ink on my blank white canvas
I keep trying to dab it off but it smudges
It grows bigger and uglier and
darker the longer I stare at it
I leave it alone for a while but it still hangs on my wall
Only making it more permanent
I look at all my other paintings
Flowers, rivers, even buildings
illuminating the horizon
They make me remember how to appreciate artwork
What my collection was before
Imperfect but not lacking
I look at all of the brush strokes
I study every piece in hopes the studio
will return to what it once was
But when I'm done gazing
My vision always circles back to the black ink stain
Ugly and abnormal and conspicuous
I should throw it out
Toss it in the nearest trash can
Toss it into the closest lake
But even if I do
I will always remember how it ruined my gallery
I will always remember that ink stain
on my blank white canvas

Pt. II

I seem to be spilling ink on many of my canvases
I have a collection
Some are stained red, others blue, even black
They are tucked into a dark little corner in my studio
I wonder how it happens sometimes
I'll get ready to apply oil paints to my canvas
Preparing to paint a bird or a carnation or a waterfall
Then my elbow hits the ink pot
Or I accidentally shake the table
Or the cat knocks it over
And just like that my painting ceases to exist
My idea will never come to fruition
I never even write letters
I don't even own a quill
Why do I mix ink with paint?
Though wouldn't it be an inconvenience
to throw out perfectly good ink?
Maybe I should let it continue to
destroy all of my artwork
And taint the aesthetic of my gallery
That's what makes the most sense
Right?

Passion dictates how wretched or
beautiful your work is
Do not worry about how it looks to others
They will understand how you feel
I know this to be true
For I do not write people letters
I send them paintings instead
And every time they send me one back

I served my weaknesses to you on a silver platter
But whose fault is it that you decided to dine?

Pt. II

Just because you were at a restaurant
It doesn't mean you needed to read the menu

If your friendship did nothing for me
Your absence will do me wonders

~ Close the door on your way out

I fear sadness more than spiders or a
burnt out bulb in my nightlight
Every time I cry a laugh escapes my lips
When my stomach gets butterflies I
never fail to take out my net
When I hear the sound of my heart
weeping into its pillow again
I frantically sing it a lullaby
I can't stand the thought of feeling normal
When the taste of joy has previously
coated my tongue

One day
When the box of Pandora is finally closed
And its contents are safely inside
You'll rediscover it
Tucked away in the attic of your mind
Behind a burnt out candle
And an ancient encyclopedia
You will draw pictures
In the dust that coats it so heavily
And revel in the fact
That the horrors within
Will never escape again

Sometimes
You just need to French braid your hair
Still damp with the salt water
The ocean used for your baptism
Stand on the top of a tall windy hill
And let the tears fall from your tired eyes
Allow them to water the grass
And penetrate the dirt
Maybe then something can grow
From the seed of happiness inside
That you thought was dead a long time ago

What power you possess my child
It is up to you how you harness it
Just never forget its presence

~ Words of wisdom

I need you to know that you are worthy
Of the crown you wear
Just because they tell you it isn't there
It does not make it any less tangible

~ The best queens are born as peasants

If you see my light on at 2AM
Know that I am going through something
I don't care to admit
Know that my only confidant in that moment
Is my pen and paper
I am scribing my darkest thoughts
And whispering my deepest secrets
So if you see my light on at 2AM
Think twice about knocking
Because I cannot guarantee
Who you'll find beyond that door

The Canvas

As I tip my head back with laughter
My mother stops and looks at me
Smiling
She mentions how good it is to see me this way
I ask her what she means
I have always seen your light
She says
But never has it shone this brightly
It is so nice to see you so happy

~ After I left

I didn't know freedom was my middle name
Until I looked at my birth certificate

On the outside
I may look like the same caterpillar
Who hopelessly wished for her wings to appear
Every day for two decades
But inside
I am now a monarch butterfly
That has fluttered
To Mexico and back dozens of times
For her annual migration

~ Subtle transformation

Don't be surprised when you borrow my blue pen
And red liquid spills out on the page

Pt. II
If you decide to stab me in the back
Your eyes shouldn't widen when
my shirt is stained blue
And your knife turns into a quill

When I finally work up the courage
to put on a nice dress
And buy my first bottle of perfume
I hope he knows how much strength it takes
To walk out that door begging the universe
To stop me from tripping
On my way down the sidewalk

I write your name in the steam on
the glass door in my shower
Just like you
It doesn't stick around when I decide to get dressed

To be undesired
Is to fall from the sky
Knowing your instructor didn't give you a parachute
On the way down from the plane

~ Free falling

How can someone so beautiful
Be so arrogant
As to assume I would blindly follow his directions
When I could just use my compass instead?

~ Get your own map

If you think you're too good to call me your own
Just remember how silly your name sounds
Coming out of someone else's mouth
I could have made it sound regal
But you chose colloquialism instead

All I want is for someone to pick me up in his arms
And hold me until my heart stops skipping beats
And my breathing becomes steady
That could have been you
But I guess I was too heavy for you to lift
Or maybe you just weren't strong enough
To carry the featherlight weight
Of my presence

~ Renew your gym membership

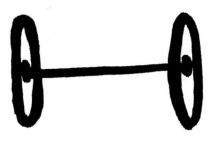

What a liar you are *Adonis*
Just because your face was carved from marble
And your eyes could stop a war
It doesn't mean you can act like a god
When all you are is a mortal
Wishing for a goddess to praise you from her alter

~ Step down from your pedestal

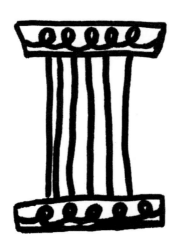

I was a falsetto
You were a note that fell flat
I tried to save you
But it ruined our symphony

In a world full of 8 billion people
How could not even one of them
Want to love every piece of me?

How can you say you love me
When you didn't attend my high school
Or hold my hand in the hallway as
you walk me to my classes?
How can you say I'm your everything
When I locked myself in my dorm
And cried on my first night away from home
Without you there to soak up my tears?
How can you call yourself my soulmate
When you haven't even arrived yet?

~ Hurry up

I am impatient to give you the
love I know you deserve
I toss and turn in my sleep
Restless in waiting to give you every piece of me
I can't wait to serve you breakfast
in bed every morning
Without even leaving the bedroom

To get drunk off of your cologne is the
only intoxication I will ever need
The only club I will ever hit up is
our living room at 2am
To look over my shoulder and see you
staring at me from across the kitchen
As I cut vegetables and you wash the dishes
Is the only time I will ever let a handsome
stranger ask me to dance
Don't you get it?
The only crazy night I want to
relive over and over again
Is last Tuesday after my pyjamas were
on and your shift was over

~ To the man I haven't met yet

Kiss me in the library
So that I may drown in the blessings
of each disembodied voice
Whispering their approval from
the ancient wooden shelves
Maybe one day
I too will be nothing but ink on paper
Willingly bound to the outcome etched
into the piles of parchment
And hidden between layers of dust and taut leather
Oh how I would love to be condemned
To living happily ever after with you
For all of eternity

Exhaustion hangs off every part of my body
Yet you still ask if I want to dance
You know I can't say no to you
So I fall in line with your movements
And savour every drop of grace
That drips from your shoulders onto the marble floor
Like echinacea honey into yogurt
Only when your hands are on my waist
When your breath glides slowly
down the length of my neck
Do I awaken instantaneously
And remember every step and turn we always take
While the crowd watches in total captivation
You are the only one who can convince me to move
When I feel incapable of rhythm

I don't think you realize how
comfortable you make me feel
When I used to flinch every time a man looked at me
And my trust in your sex was unable
to be further diminished
I like you
And that is something I never thought I could do

I used to get on my knees every night
Asking the universe to grant me your presence
And bless me with my twisted fantasies
How ironic that now
I get on my knees every evening
To worship you like you were never gone
And I didn't have to beg for you to come

When he kisses me
It feels like everything in the world makes sense
Like I could pick up quantum
physics in a single afternoon
Or identify how many molecules
there are in a flower petal
Just by looking at it
He makes science seem simple
And makes math appear mediocre
He is a data management class
with a patient professor
And I am ready to study

You compliment my nails like my
technician did you a favour
Only when I scratch them down
your back six hours later
Do I understand why your eyes lit
up at the sight of the polish

~ Nasty

The only time I let my legs go numb
from the words a man speaks to me
Is from pure uninhibited desire
When we're behind a locked door
Beneath a warm comforter
And your hands are showing me all the ways
We can be intertwined in our physical attraction

~ Weakness

How can they tell me that getting older
Is something to dread
When my childhood brought with it
More nightmares than any tax evasion or student loan
Could ever cause me?

They tell her to age like a fine wine
Whose hues and bouquets ripen
over time in the cellar
They can't wait to get their hands on the glass stems
So they can sip the rich and silky liquid
that comes with maturation
The liquor saved only for special occasions
And celebrations of countless milestones
They pay $200 just to hold the bottle in their hands
Boasting to their snobby cohorts
About what they went through to afford her presence
How they bought a new corkscrew
Because the seal is only fit to be removed
by a gold ordained mechanism
She can only be served slightly chilled
Otherwise you risk spoiling
The infusions of bergamot and black cherry
Which were steeped for exactly 22 minutes
Then kept in the left
Not right
Syrah of the vineyard
Oh yes
She ages like a fine wine
She ages like a fine wine whose wooden barrel
Rotted half way through the aging process
She ages like a fine wine that has
been mixed with saliva
On occasion by a greedy chambermaid

She ages like a fine wine that sat
in the sun for 12 hours
And whose fermentation was
complete about seven years ago
She ages like a fine wine that has been tampered with
Tainted and intoxicated with the poison of worry
And the elixir of growing up too quickly
She is a fine wine who has survived everything
From termites to toxins to taste testers
But still insists on being exquisite

~ 20 year old Merlot

I ask her
Why must I always be on the verge of tears?
The answer is obvious my child
She tells me
For to be a poet is to have the universe fill
you with so much passion for life
That you are one drop away from overflowing
Every second you're alive

I have only dipped my toe into the pool of poetry
But I intend to jump off of the high dive

I always knew how to paint landscapes
But when the brush is constantly
snatched from your hands
And your paint always somehow gets spilled
There will never be a single piece of art in your home
Until you decide to get your own apartment

~ Become your own studio

Acknowledgments

Gosh, I don't know where to start! This collection means the world to me. It is how I got through a really difficult period in my life that I never thought I would see the other side of. I am elated to be able to share it with the world as my debut poetry collection. I would like to thank my mom, Lynda Cork, for her overwhelming support and encouragement throughout not only this process, but my entire life. She always told me that if I wanted to do something, it's only a matter of putting in the effort and believing that it will come to fruition. Her endless praise and pride in my dreams has made me have confidence in my abilities as a writer, and that is the greatest gift I could have ever received as her daughter. She deserves an award for being the best mother on the planet, and that is no exaggeration I can assure you. I love you Mum. Thank you to my Grandma and Grandpa for encouraging me through my writing process, even if they don't understand my poems. My metaphors escape them, but their love for me never goes unfelt. Thank you to my favourite high school English teacher, Ms. Helsby – oops, I mean Amy! You truly changed my life and you gave me the courage to make the hardest decision I've ever made. You were my safe haven when I felt the most anxious, and you pushed me into becoming the writer I am today. *Thank you* doesn't even begin to cover it. Thank you to my best friends for always believing and encouraging me in whatever I do, picking me up when I feel down, and for supporting my poetry. I was embarrassed to write for a long time, but never once did you make me feel ashamed when I started sharing it with you. You are my sisters for life, and thank you for giving me your money to support the release of this book, haha. Thank you to my other friends who also support me in my writing and for buying my book. I love you guys so much and I live for those deep conversations we have in the most random of places and times. Thank you to Tellwell for making my dream of becoming a published and well-known author and poet come true. I am forever grateful for your help. Thank you to the Universe. Manifestation is real, and it always, always works. Finally, thank you to anyone who chooses to pick up this book and read my words, and especially every girl like me who is struggling in silence with a smile on their face. To the girls who feel like they will never escape. To the girls who wonder every day if their dreams are even possible for someone in their position. Trust me, they are. It truly means the most to me that you are willing to support me and find a home in between these pages. Thank you for feeling something while your eyes scan these pages. Thank you for spending your free time with me and my mind. Thank you for taking refuge in my poems. Thank you for your love. You are why I write, and there is SO much more to come. Trust the process, and always keep writing. See you soon.

Olivia Kosmo ♡

About the Author

Olivia Kosmo is a 20 year old Greek Canadian author and poet. She loves to read romance novels, drink tea, and romanticize her life as much as possible. She studies at Trent University with a major in English Literature, and is working towards pursuing a career as an English teacher. This is Olivia's first independently published poetry collection, though she has previously published her work in Trent University's student writing anthology *Chickenscratch*. She is always writing to keep her creativity flowing and her fans entertained.